I LOVE BAD WEATHER DAYS

BAD WEATHER ACTIVITIES

BRENDA LEE THOMAS

ILLUSTRATED BY MATS SNALLFOT

AuthorHouse™
1663 Liberty Drive
Bloomington, IN 47403
www.authorhouse.com
Phone: 1-800-839-8640

Published by AuthorHouse 04/29/2014

ISBN: 978-1-4969-0763-9 (sc)
ISBN: 978-1-4969-0764-6 (e)

Any people depicted in stock imagery provided by Thinkstock are models, and such images are being used for illustrative purposes only.
Certain stock imagery © Thinkstock.

This book is printed on acid-free paper.

Because of the dynamic nature of the Internet, any web addresses or links contained in this book may have changed since publication and may no longer be valid. The views expressed in this work are solely those of the author and do not necessarily reflect the views of the publisher, and the publisher hereby disclaims any responsibility for them.

authorHOUSE®

Table of Contents

Dedications.. i

Special Thanks... i

Shout Outs!!!! i

The Artist iii

Story: I Love Bad Weather Days.......................5

Lesson Plan Topic: Weather...........................35

Parent and Child Homework...........................36

Emergency Weather Kit List...........................38

Group Time Activity......................................39

Poem... 40

PORTRAITS OF CHILDREN...........................41

Enlighten Training Program 42

Please Support The Breast Cancer Scociety 43

Please Support The American Red Cross 44

Dedications

Without speaking or writing a word; a great dedication goes out to my very loving and supported mother **Hilda Thibodeaux Thomas**. I also give special thanks to my siblings Barbara Jean Thomas, Clinton Thomas Jr., Billy Ray Thomas and Gary Mark Thomas; for prays and constructed feedback.

This book is dedicated to all the children in my hometown Beaumont TX. And to all the children in the world that will need to evacuate, because of bad weather.

Special Thanks

Special thanks to **Sibyl McDade**, for taking my flyer off the bulletin board, in the break room; and giving it to her son-n-law Mats Snallfot.

Special thanks to **Mats**; for taking my words and putting pictures to them.

Special thanks to **Diana Trevino**; for taking time out of her busy life to read and edit my book.

Shout Outs!!!!

I want to give a shout out to my nieces (Desiree Denise Rivers, Miracle Taylor Thomas, Mya Porter and Aliyah Porter) for reading my book and giving helpful feedback.

And to all my smart nephews (Solomon Dwayne Thomas, Joshua Thomas Rivers and Gray Mark Thomas Jr.) for helping with technology advise.

The Artist

I want to thank Mats; for drawing the pictures for this great book. His fantastic art work, will help me teach children about bad weather conditions. Please take time to visit his website; and see his great creations.

~Mattsen77
Mats
Artist | Hobbyist | Varied
United States
Swedish guy currently living in Austin TX
Been drawing since I was a kid.

Inspiration was my cousin Jonny Nordlund who became the youngest Comic book artist in Sweden with "91:an".
Amazing artist!
As far as other artists that has inspired me-Too many to mention, but one that comes to mind right away is Frank Miller. A recent favorite is Patrick Brown (patrickbrown.deviantart.com/)

My style varies, but I tend to mostly do simple style comic-book stuff.
Have done some work illustrating a few books, CD albums and various greeting cards etc- mostly for family.

This is just a really quick Bio, may update more later.

http://mattsen77.deviantart.com/

My name is Desiree' and I love having fun every day, but my favorite days of the year are bad weather days. My sister Janice hates bad weather days; because she said there is nothing to do.

Janice is 10 years old and I think she is too old to have fun on the best days of the year. She thinks all the fun happens when it's warm and sunny; but I know we can have fun every day.

I love sunny days also, because I can read books, play on the playground, run in the park, climb trees and pick flowers. I love riding my scooter, roller skating and playing sports with my family; but the most fun takes place on bad weather days.

I love all the things I can do when it's raining. I love getting in a box and pretending I am a captain of a fishing boat, floating down the river fishing. I get excited when my friends and I read a story together and then bring the story alive by becoming the characters in the story. One day when my dad and I were walking home from the park it began to rain, so we decided to make it fun, and we began singing in the rain.

Sometimes we just sit on the steps and watch the rain fall on the buildings, trees and grass. All the noise stops and everyone are captured by the sounds of nature; everything becomes calm and sleepy from the sounds of the rain. My friends and I love lying on a blanket, listening to a story on a DVD. Soon we are lulled to sleep by the sound of rain.

Cold, freezing days are really cool for me. I like putting on my long-johns, socks, shirt, sweater, bluejeans, coat, gloves, hat, earmuffs and boots. Sometimes I have on so many winter items that I fall down backward on the floor.

When I finally get outdoors, I like walking, slipping and sliding on the frozen grass and sidewalk. My mother said I am just like a yoyo, going up and down.

When I arrive at my Head Start classroom; my teacher, Ms. Francis, says it's time to peel the banana, and we both laugh. My teacher helps me take off my jacket, but I take off my hat, gloves, earmuffs, sweater and boots.

On cold days, when it's too cold to go outdoors, we make warm chocolate milk and listen to Ms. Francis read our favorite stories. Then after nap, we get to play instruments that make sounds you hear on a cold winter day. One cold day, Ms. Francis let us make our own mittens. We drew our hands on felt material, punched holes on the edges of the front and back sides, and then sewed them together with yarn. My friends and I said we will wear our mittens to school every day.

Everyone at my school dreams of windy days, because we get to do fun things. When the wind is moving fast, it moves everything around outdoors. We see the plants, leaves, paper, clothes and small objects moving; it's fun to see all those things flying around in the air. Ms. Francis said we will look at the colors of the wind. Today we will paint with the colors of the wind in the art area.

Ms. Francis shared a story about a long time ago when she was younger. The wind from a hurricane blew her all the way from her job back to her house; and that was the only day she missed work. My friend Rebecca said the hurricane must have read Ms. Francis's mind, because Ms. Francis always says the best place to be on a cold, windy day is in your bed. I would have loved to see Ms. Francis fly in the air with the birds.

We begged Ms. Francis to go outside, because we wanted to see her fly home. Rebecca said she hopes Ms. Francis flies to the store for some paint, because the bottles are empty. Then Ms. Francis said that we all will be flying today, we screamed and jumped with joy and began saying, "we're going to fly in the air, we're going to fly in the air."

Ms. Francis finally explained to us that we are going to make kites; each of us will draw our picture on our kite and then open the door and let it loose in the wind. We really wanted to fly, but were excited about making a kite and drawing ourselves.

When all the kites were ready, Ms. Francis said if the wind blows her into the tree, we are to get Ms. Shuler to help her out of the tree. My friend Rebecca said that we should call the Fire Department and they will get Mrs. Francis out of the tree like they get cats out of trees.

Ms. Francis gathered the kites and asked us all to sit by the large window in our classroom so that we could see her fight the wind. When she opened the door, the wind was so strong that it blew all the art paper and baskets onto the floor.

Ms. Francis made it outdoors safely, but her jacket was moving fast, like wings, and her hair was dancing on her head. She made it to the tree and held on and began walking toward the wall, but the wind knocked her down. Everyone screamed, "Get up Ms. Francis, get up Ms. Francis." Ms. Francis grabbed the tree and pulled herself up; everyone yelled, "Yea Ms. Francis." She walked toward the wall and taped all the kites onto the fence, then hurried back to the classroom.

Ms. Francis said, "The wind is strong; it almost took me away." She said, "Everyone please watch the kites." The kites flew back and forth, back and forth and then all the kites flew away, a few at a time. We were all excited to see each other fly away in the wind.

Ms. Francis asked the class to sit down for group time discussion. Ms. Francis said "Now it's time to learn about dangerous weather and what we can do to be calm, helpful and safe. Dangerous weathers are hurricanes, tornadoes, snow storms and very hot temperatures."

"What is a hurricane?," asked Desiree. Ms. Francis said, "A hurricane is a very strong and powerful wind with heavy rain, moving very fast; it can hurt and destroy things in its path. The water that the hurricanes bring sometimes floods people's homes, cars and businesses. When a hurricane is in the area, everyone needs to be on high, level land in a strong building, or out of the area."

  "What is a tornado?," asked Rebecca. Ms. Francis said, "A tornado is a funnel-shaped, rotating column of air that passes in a narrow path over land, moving and destroying objects and people. When a tornado is in the area everyone needs to be in a safe, strong building, in a room where there are no windows, or out of the area."

Ms. Francis continued, "Children a snow storm is when heavy snow falls down and covers the yards, houses, streets and cars. When there is a snow storm, it's important that you stay warm, by wearing warm clothes and remaining in a warm place, eating warm foods and drinks."

"Class, we all know the last dangerous weather is too much heat. The temperature can get so hot that anything can easily start a large fire. A fire destroys everything it touches. The best place to be when the outdoor temperature is very high is in a cool place and away from fire."

Ms. Francis said, "there are three important things I want you to remember: be calm, helpful and safe."

"First, Ms. Francis said "please try to be calm. You must be quiet and listen to the person who is taking care of you. That may be your parents, a relative, teacher, friend or the responsible person who is taking care of you. Only a calm person can listen and follow directions; they will know what to do in dangerous weather.

Three quick things you can do that will help you stay calm: A- Take a few deep breaths letting each breath out slowly;

B- Try drinking cold water; C- Think about something that makes you happy, like your favorite activity, movie or friend.

"Second, be helpful; A- Follow directions; B- Help each other, especially someone younger or an elderly adult; C- Stay together and help other people stay calm.

"Third, stay safe; A- Move away from windows and doors; B- Find a safe place to protect yourself from flying or falling objects; C- Listen for sounds that may indicate danger, such as outdoor furniture being blown around, doors banging, glass breaking, etc....

"Class our group project today is making a safety kit. This kit will come in handy when there is a dangerous weather on the way; you and your family will need to pack and move to a shelter or out of the city. Everyone will be given a bag, flashlight, book, band-aids, and a bottle of water, a bag of dry fruit, a book, papers, colors and one board game. I also have some things your parents could add to the list. Please keep this kit prepared and in a place that's easy to find when dangerous weather is in the area.

"When dangerous weather is in the area we must know what to do so we can be calm, helpful and safe; but there are bad weather days that can be fun, educational and exciting."

I wish my sister Janice would love bad weather days. I think I will change the name to "Better Days," yes, "Better Days." I love the better days of the year.

I am writing a list of things I can do on bad weather days; you and your friends should make a list too and post it on the wall, so when a bad weather day comes along, you'll have fun things to do at school and at home.

I enjoy Bad Weather Days at home and at school, because it's not what the day brings, but what *you* bring to the day. Next time it's raining, windy or freezing cold, think of something fun and exciting you can do on that day. I know one fun thing you can do on any day, and that's read a book.

I wrote a song and I want you to sing it with me;

"We're all in this weather together"

We're all in this weather together; we're all in this weather together, so let's have some fun. We're all in this weather together, we're all in this weather together, we're all in this weather together, so let's have some fun. On rainy days you can look out the window and watch the rain water the plants and wash the earth. On windy days you can fly your kites and troubles away. On cold days you can heat up with chocolate and make some mittens to warm your hands. Ask a friend to help you have a fun day, because we're all in this together, no matter what the weather.

Lesson Plan Topic: Weather

Weekdays	Learning Centers	Transition	PEP	Outdoors	Afternoon	Special Needs
Monday **Sunny Days** Circle Time **Book**: I Love Bad Weather Days **Letter** "W"	**Science:** Plant seeds in different soils **Writing:** The children will collage and write the letter W	**Song** **Book** **Game** **Charade** **Finger play**	**Cognitive:** Match different flower seeds **Gross Motor:** see outdoors	Ride bike, **Writing: children will write the letter "W" in the dirt or sand**	**Health:** **Exercise** **Book**: _W___	**Mental Health:** Plant flower seeds to take home
Tuesday **Rainy Days** Circle Time: Have things that the rain helps us with **Volunteer**: have a weather man come and give the weather prediction from the school **Letter: W**	**Art:** Paint while listening to rain music **Library:** Act out story **Water Play:** The children will sink or float seeds	**Song** **Game** **Story** **Finger play**	**Language:** see library **Fine Motors Skills:** See Art	**Science: Observe the different textures of dry sand and wet sand**	**Group Time:** Things that start with a "W" **Blocks:** The children will make a boat	**Table Games:** Weather Bingo
Wednesday **Windy Days** Circle Time: Show a 10 minute DVD on the wind. **Book**:_____	**Construction:** Make kites, draw self **Blocks:** Have the children try to move things by blowing through a straw	**Group Time** **Game** **Charade** **Song** **Book**	**Cognitive:** see Blocks **Gross Motor:** See outdoors	**Make Wind Strings for the trees** **Game:** Teacher will label things that start with "W" children will find words	**Art: Paint using the colors of things that fly on windy days.** **Book: I Love Bad Weather Days**	**Health:** **Group Time:** Exercise
Thursday **Cold Days** Circle Time: Observe different temperature of ice and water **Book**: _____	**Cooking:** chicken soup. **Construction:** Make mittens using felt and yarn	**Group Time:** **Book** **Song** **Finger play**	**Socialization** See Cooking **Cognitive:** See Construction	**Game: 1,2,3 FREEZE**	**Music: play instrument** **Book**: ____	**Nutrition:** Chicken. soup provides protein **Writing:** Write the "W" on paper
Friday Dangerous Weather Circle Time: Movie on Weather **Book**: _____	**Dramatic Play:** Set up like a shelter **Table games:** Weather matching game	**Book** **Game:** Weather **Song** We all in this weather	**Gross Motor:** See Circle Time **Fine Motor:** See Table Games	**Game: Basketball**	**Group Activity: Act out words that start with "W"**	**Library:** I Love Bad Weather Days

Parent and Child Homework

Parents, this week we will be discussing the topic "Weather". We recognized that we are a partner in your child's education and would like you to help us teach this topic to your child. Our book for the week is "I Love Bad Weather Days" by Brenda Lee Thomas. Please feel free to check this book out in your local library or purchase it at bookstores or on line.

Your child's assignment this week will be to make a list of fun things to do on bad weather days, then share one activity with the class during group time. And if you live in an area where there is high probability of dangerous weathers, please take time to make a Bad Weather Safety Kit for you and your children; please look at the attached list; it will help you put together your kit. Also make an escape route for your home. Put it on a poster, in several places then practice using that route at least once each season.

To help your child learn about the tools and items needed for bad weather days, please play the game "Weather Charade" with your family.

Weather Charade Word List

Umbrella

Coat

Hat

Sunglasses

Gloves or Mitten

Scarf

Long-johns

Raincoat

Sweater

Boots

Shorts

Rain

Snow

Wind

Sun

Socks

Skates

Field Trips for the family that will enhance your child's learning about the topic.

Park

Ice Factory

Museums

Creek

Wind Field

Weather Station

Botanical Garden

Emergency Weather Kit List

Water

All sizes band-aids

Antibiotic Cream

Books

Family and Friends' Phone Numbers

Pencils

Crayons

Cell Phone

Phone Charger

Blanket

Change of clothes

Hygiene Items

Towels

Hats

Socks

Personal items

Canned Food

Snacks

Games

Radio

IPods

Computer

DVD

DVD Player

Group Time Activity

Please allow each child the opportunity to share their fun activity for bad weather days. You may want to start on a Wednesday; this will give every child a chance to bring and share their activity. Make a book of all the ideas the children have shared and send it home on Friday. Get parents to help with typing, cutting, coloring or whatever is needed to make this book fun and usable. Please remember to put each child's name on their activity, and if a child didn't return their homework, get a volunteer to help them think of a simple idea. Repetitions may occur, and that is fine, because most repetitions will have different details. Have fun doing the activities and don't forget to invite the families to volunteer when it's their child's turn to share their idea for bad-weather fun.

Poem

Write Out Your Day

The day is as a blank sheet of paper,
waiting to be filled by actions of busy, creative people.
We each have our own paper
 and we can mark on it what we want.
Let us write out our day,
 putting our creative marks on the world.
Choose this day to fill your paper
 with fun, creative, exciting and positive events.

Brenda Lee Thomas

PORTRAITS OF CHILDREN

Children are portraits of what they see.
Yet sometimes we are embarrassed
when we don't like what they do.

Children are recorders
of the words we say.
Yet we discipline them
when they use inappropriate language.

Children are our future.
Yet we are sometimes ashamed
when they repeat our past.

What you do, what you say
and where you go
paints the picture of a child's mind.

Brenda Lee Thomas

2004

Enlighten Training Program

We provide Child Development Training
for
Head Start Programs and Childcare Centers

We are available for onsite training on Saturdays

Time: 9:00 a.m. – 12:00 p.m.

Or

Time: 1:00 p.m. – 4:00 p.m.

Price: $50.00 a person
40.00 a person if the training takes place at your location

The price is subject to change; please ask for current prices.

Make arrangement early for your program today.
Must be a group of ten or more
We will work with your schedule.

Contact

CEO: Brenda Thomas

512-577-3538

We will turn the light on for some and brighten it for others!

Please Support The Breast Cancer Scociety

Email Patient Support: support@breastcancersociety.org
Public: info@breastcancersociety.org
Phone (888) 470-7909 Locations Fax (480) 659-9807
Headquarters The Breast Cancer Society, Inc. 6859

East Rembrandt Ave., Ste. 128 Mesa, AZ 85212

**Please Support
The American Red Cross**

National Red Cross

**American Red Cross National Headquarters
2025 E. Street, NW
Washington, DC 20006
1-800-Red Cross
(1-800-733-2767)
National Headquarters Staff Directory
202-303-5214**

Gary Mark Thomas Jr.
Thanks for your support and advice.

Back Row: Desiree Denise Rivers and Joshua Thomas Rivers
Front Row: Aliyah Porter, Mya Porter and Miracle Taylor Thomas

Thanks for your support and advice.

Printed in the United States
by Baker & Taylor Publisher Services